30 More Tips
To Unlock Your
Potential

BEN GLENN

BUILDING
SUCCESS

BRICK by BRICK

Building Success Brick By Brick, Volume 2
Copyright (c) 2012 by Ben Glenn

Cover design by Cara Tudor

Library of Congress Cataloging-in-Publication Data

Glenn, Ben
   Building Success Brick by Brick, Volume 2 / Ben Glenn
      p. cm.
Includes biographic reference
ISBN 978-0-9675680-7-2 (paperback)
1. Teen Issues
2. Inspiration
3. Self Help

I. Glenn, Ben   II. Title

Library of Congress Catalog Card Number: 2012951504

TABLE OF CONTENTS

TABLE OF CONTENTS (continued)

TABLE OF CONTENTS (continued)

Introduction

BUILDING SUCCESS

Seven Ways To Achieve Your Potential with Plastic Toy Bricks

"Play is our brain's favorite way of learning."
– Diane Ackerman

When I was a kid, I spent hours at a time in a pile of LEGO building bricks, constructing cars, boats, planes, and spaceships. It was my own little world made out of thousands of interlocking pieces. I was crazy about LEGOs. Forget swimming in a pit of plastic balls; fill it with LEGOs and let me dive right in! (On second thought, ouch.)

Honestly, I still love LEGOs, and I'll pick up a cool-looking set from time to time. I recently realized that LEGOs can do more than let me build whatever my imagination comes up with. They can teach me to build myself up to be the kind of person that I want to be.

Once I started thinking about it, the parallels between building colorful toy spaceships and building a successful life snapped together. I don't know if I can think of a more playful teaching tool to encourage you to achieve focus, stay on track, and move forward in life. So, with LEGOs on the brain, I'd like to share my observations and things I've learned over the last 20 years spent speaking, drawing, and just trying to live the best life I can.

While reading this, I recommend that you grab a few LEGOs to play with. It'll be a fun way to remember that success isn't something you're born with, and it doesn't happen overnight. You build it, brick by brick.

Plates : **Finding the foundation for success**

"Deep meaning lies often in childish play." – Johann Friedrich von Schiller, German poet

Let's say that you've got your LEGO set out, and you want a build a big apple – even better, how about THE Big Apple, New York City? You'll start with plates. Plates are the foundation for your model, and they determine what you can build, how big you can build it, and how sturdy it will be. The same is true when building a successful life; you need to start with a strong foundation.

With LEGOs, you typically begin with the largest plate as the core foundation, and then smaller plates are added. This large plate is the most important piece of the model because everything builds upon it. It provides stability and structure.

To be successful, you also need a core foundation to build your life upon. My core is the plate of attitude, which is how I think or feel. Attitude is fundamental it provides stability and structure to how I behave in every situation.

Upon attitude, I attach the plate of faith, a belief in myself, God, and others. Then I add optimism, working to always think positive. Finally, I attach vision, which is thinking big, dreaming big, and working to keep success in sight.

With all of my plates in place, I have a solid foundation, and that's the crucial first step to building success!

Bricks: The Construction of Character

Once the plates are in place, it's time to attach bricks. Bricks come in a variety of shapes and sizes. You can choose to arrange them in one of countless ways. When building a successful life, character qualities are your bricks, and you can choose what qualities define your character, which is what makes you a unique individual. So, you're sitting with a heaping pile of LEGOs of all different kinds. How do you know which bricks to choose? You consult your vision for the model – the picture in your mind of what you want to build. For now, let's stay with New York City. If you want to build the Empire State Building, you'll probably pick a lot of gray bricks with blue or white bricks for windows. For the Statue of Liberty, you might go with green with some yellow for her torch.

Your vision for a successful life – your goals and dreams – will guide which character qualities you choose. For example, if your vision for success says that you should be humble, then you should select a brick of Humility and stack it on your foundation. Picking a brick of Bragging wouldn't fit in your vision; leave that one in the pile.

When people fail to consult their vision, they just take on character qualities at random. That leads nowhere near success. If you've stacked LEGO bricks with no plan, you know that it leads to an unstable and unidentifiable mess.

Think before you pick, and success will start to take form!

2 KEY QUESTIONS:

- **What is your vision of success?**
- **What are the qualities you need to achieve that vision of success?**

Pieces in Pairs:
Keeping Your Balance.

When you pour a new box of LEGOs out on the table, you'll notice that pieces typically come in even numbers: two windows, four wheels, eight plates, and so on. This is to give the model balance. If you're building a car and you only have three wheels, one corner of the car can drag. In the same way, a successful life needs balance.

For example, if you choose a brick of strength, then you should add a brick of humility to balance it out. Note that strength and humility aren't opposites, but they complement each other. A strong person should be humble so that they don't become boastful with their strength. Or if you choose humor, then balance it with sensitivity to keep your jokes from offending or hurting people.

Without balance, our model for success will have good qualities that go too far. Confident people might become conceited. Funny people could turn obnoxious. And just like a model plane with only one wing, the whole thing falls over.

Keep your balance and keep building!

Opportunities:
Your Definition of Success May Change

I've loved LEGOs since I was a kid, and they just keep getting better! New kinds of bricks come out all the time. My imagination is stretched by the ever-evolving possibilities of what I can build. A successful life keeps up with changes and new opportunities, too.

LEGOs evolve in all sorts of ways: new colors, bricks that move in new ways, and new sets. There's a Space Shuttle set now, but there wasn't when LEGOs started in the 1940s – because there wasn't a Space Shuttle in the 1940s! And good luck finding a Harry Potter set from the '80s! (Harry's first book came out in '97.)

As you build your successful life, watch for new opportunities. Maybe you'll try playing the guitar and realize that you like it. So, you might add musician to your definition of the person you want to be. Or perhaps you'll move to Colorado and fall in love with rock climbing. Or wouldn't it be cool if you enrolled into that wizard school that opened up down the street? (The last Harry Potter reference, I promise!) You never know what fun and exciting opportunity lies around the corner, so keep watching!

Rebuilding: Don't Be Afraid to Start Over

When building a LEGO model, sometimes you'll find that there's a better way to piece things together than you first thought. It's not that there was a problem with your original vision; you just can't predict every trouble spot before it comes up. Your best option is to break it apart and rebuild. A model for success can benefit from rebuilding, too.

Maybe your car model would look better in red than in blue. Or your Empire State Building leans a lot like that famous tower in Pisa. Recently, I had a decent airplane in the works until I realized that it just wasn't going to turn out the way I planned. I took it apart, and now I have a Noah's Ark that floats my boat.

A successful life takes note of what's not working. If you're trying to exercise, you might realize that you just don't enjoy running. So, you try swimming instead. Maybe you realized that your college major isn't some thing that you'd actually like to do. Or you may really want to be Champion of the Westminster Dog Show, but you're not a dog.

Starting over might feel like failure, but you're actually learning that there's a better way to reach your goal. And learning is a good thing.

There's more than one way to success, so feel free to rebuild!

Perseverance:
Success Keeps Moving

If you walk through the LEGO section at the store, you'll notice that most of the models are vehicles: cars, trains, planes, and more. First you build it and then you move it; some models even move themselves! Your model of success needs to keep moving, too, especially when it feels like life is stuck at a standstill.

When I was a kid, there were many times when I wanted to throw a LEGO model against a wall — not because I was building a LEGO tennis ball, but because I was frustrated that I couldn't get it to turn out the way I wanted. However, I'm glad that I didn't give in to frustration, because I would have missed out on creating some very cool models.

In a successful life, perseverance is the act of pushing through when you could just give up out of frustration or anger. In the face of challenge, you dig deep and tap into your inner motivation, discipline, and self-control. This could be finishing a tough project for school or working through a rough patch in your marriage.

I love how Bill Hybels said, "Most people quit when the finish line is just right around the corner."

Keep moving forward and you'll reach the finish line eventually. You'll be glad that you did!

Play: A Celebration

What's my motivation for building with LEGOs? It's FUN! I love envisioning a model in my mind and then actually creating it with my cherished plastic toy bricks. It can be hard work, but it gives me a sense of accomplishment and satisfaction. And when I was younger, I took my new creations and played with them for hours. As we get older, we forget the benefits that come from playing. We get so wrapped up in work, money, and status that forget to celebrate with play. Play is a time to rest from your work and enjoy life. It can also be a time to open your mind to new visions and find a spark of motivation for the next challenge.

A successful life needs play. Enjoy your success Rejoice in your journey and all that you've built, all that you've learned and all that you've become.

There will always be building to be done, so you might as well play on a regular basis!

> *"You cannot dream yourself into a character; you must hammer and forge yourself one."*
> *— Henry David Thoreau*

Building with LEGOs is a process, and I love that. You pull them out of the box, and you have to work before you can play. With most toys, the only work you have to do is snip off 100 twist-ties (which is no easy task). LEGO models need to be built, and that takes hours. A successful life also needs to be built, and that takes years. The real difference is that the reward of success lasts a lifetime.

When I open a LEGO model, I lay out all of the

pieces first, so when it comes time to add a brick, I don't have to search for it. I can get right to building. In life, many people spend too much time searching for the right pieces to add into their lives instead of actually building better lives. I want to help people stop searching and start building, so I've written this book series.

The Success Building Series is an encouraging, ADHD-friendly resource for your personal building project. My motto is "Keep It Simple!" so each book in the series is less than 100 pages, and yet jam-packed with 30 tips – one tip for each day of the month. The tips are bite-sized, and they'll playfully spark ideas and actions to help you build a better you. Phase One focuses on the foundational areas in our life, and each following Phase will build upon that foundation.

For those of you who struggle with focus (like me), you can watch these tips on You-Tube, in addition to reading them in the books.

I hope that these books will help you achieve your potential and reach success.

Enjoy Building!

Post your LEGO
creation at
 simplybenglenn
to win FREE stuff!

14

Building Success

Tips 1 through 13

teach about personal values,
stuff that's part of you.

Tips 14 to 21

teach about relating well to others.

Tips 22 through 30

teach about pursuing your goal
through a vision.

Success Building Tip 1

CHARACTER: WHO YOU ARE

Can you tell the difference between Mickey Mouse and Donald Duck? Of course! (Unless you grew up in a cave, which means you might actually be a bear. Cool, a bear who can read!) To tell the difference between Mickey and Donald, you could compare their clothes, voices, and personalities. Oh, and there's the minor detail that one is a mouse and the other is a duck! All of these features make up their character.

Character isn't just for the cartoons; it's for all of us! In real life, **character** can be defined as the combination of features or qualities that make you an individual. In other words, it's the total of all of the little things that make you who you are. That includes the obvious stuff like what you wear and how tall you are. But more importantly, it includes parts of your personality, like

- Whether you tell the truth
- If people can depend on you
- How often you help other people

To have a successful life, you need a certain kind of character. Someone who lies, steals, and cheats isn't going to be successful. That's bad character. No one will trust them, and they'll end up alienated, maybe even in prison!

If you have good character, a successful life is yours for the taking. People (or your fellow bears) will enjoy being around you. It will make them feel better about themselves and the world, in general.

In this book, I'm going to give you tips on how to build good character, and we'll start tomorrow with values. Even Mickey Mouse would agree that a successful life is more fun than a trip to Disneyland!

TIP: Having good character leads to a successful life.

Success Building Tip 2

VALUES: PRICELESS

Have you ever been to Costco, or another wholesale store, where you can buy your groceries in bulk and save money? It's amazing what you can get, like a 20-pack of Gatorade or 144 Stouffer Meatloaf dinners for $9.99. You can have a "Meat Festival!"

Getting all that food for low prices sounds like a great value. But I want to talk about a more important kind of value. (Not to say that cheap meat isn't important.)

Values are the set of morals a person has. They might be called 'values' because morals are so important and valuable to a person's life. To build a successful life, you need to know what your values are.

If you were to explain your values, you might say, "I believe that people should tell the truth." That value is called honesty. Or you might say, "I believe that someone shouldn't be late when they commit to a time. That's punctuality.

Whether you realize it or not, you have values. You believe that certain actions are right or wrong. Just think about how you'd feel if someone stole your wallet or insulted you. You'd be upset because you know that those things are wrong. Or what if someone bought you a delicious dinner, or even saved your life? You'd be happy and grateful because those reflect positive values.

This book will cover different kinds of values, like honesty and punctuality, and how they can help you build a successful life with a strong foundation. I write these tips so you can identify what things in your life you need to get rid off and what things in your life you can build upon, positive values and character. I think it's a good deal – even better than saving money on 144 frozen loaves of meat!

TIP: Define your values, so you can build on a strong foundation.

Success Building Tip 3

HONESTY, PART 1: YOU CAN HANDLE THE TRUTH!

Okay, time for a pop quiz, you math hotshots! What's 1+1? If you said 2, give yourself a congratulatory pat on the back!

But what if 1+1 didn't equal 2? What if the answer was whatever you felt like it should be, like 3 or 4 or 100? Then everything about our world would be all screwy. We wouldn't be able to measure distances or count money or find out how many licks it takes to get to the center of a Tootsie Roll Pop. So, it's a good thing that we know that 1+1=2, end of story. That's a fact; it's the truth.

Honesty is living with an attitude of telling the truth. Honesty is important to having a successful life because reality – the world as we know it – is based on the truth. If you live your life not telling the truth, you wouldn't get very far.

YOU: "Hi, my name is Fred."
ME: "Hi, Fred."

YOU: "Actually, my name is George."
ME: "Okay, um, George..."
YOU: "Well, my name is really Luke...Luke Skywalker."
ME: "Goodbye."

Don't get me wrong...I'd LOVE to meet Luke Skywalker, but I'd have a feeling that you're not him.

Honesty is the foundation of every relationship. If you can't believe what the other person says, why would you want to talk to them at all? They would be out of touch with reality. This goes for friendships, dating, jobs, and any other time you're talking with someone.

To tell you the truth, I think that you should tell the truth. It's honestly the best way to live!

TIP: Approach every conversation with honesty.

Success Building Tip

HONESTY, PART 2: LITTLE WHITE LIES ARE HUGE

"The dog ate my homework!"

I hope you never used that excuse in school. If I were your teacher, I wouldn't believe you. Unless you etched your homework on a big Milk Bone, it probably wouldn't be the truth.

That's called a 'little white lie,' a lie that you think is harmless and will get you out of an uncomfortable situation. You think that no one will get hurt. Other little white lies include:

"Oh, I was in the shower when you called."
"I guess I never got that email."
"Yes, I loved the homemade (fruitcake/cheese log/chopped liver)!"

But little white lies aren't harmless. Say that you tell Grandma that you loved the fruitcake she sent you for Christmas, when, in fact, you thought it resembled a brick of Play-Doh and gravel. You'll only have yourself to blame when you get the same fruitcake for the next 10 years.

And it's scary how easy it is to become an expert at lying. At first, you may feel guilty about telling your first little white lie. However, the more you tell them, the easier it gets. This goes on until you realize that lying doesn't bother you at all. You weave a web of lies, and then you lie about the lies, and you have to keep track of who you lied to and who you didn't so your lies aren't exposed. All that lying might seem the easy way out in the moment, but what you'll find is that managing a life of lies is exhausting. And managing a life full of little white lies isn't building toward a successful life.

So, go ahead and admit that you didn't do your homework. Or that you just forgot to reply to the email. Most people would prefer to hear the truth over what you think they want to hear. It's better than blaming your dear old dog!

TIP: *There's no such thing as a harmless lie.*

Success Building Tip 5

INTEGRITY, PART 1: ROCK SOLID

When talking about a ship, its 'integrity' refers to how solid and strong the structure is. This is important, well, because you don't want to be on a ship when it starts coming apart and sinking. The Titanic was said to have the most solid integrity ever; they called it 'unsinkable'. Unfortunately, we know how that story ended.

In terms of people, **integrity** refers to how solid and strong you are in your values. It means that you behave in a way that agrees with your moral and ethical principles. Basically, it's being who you say you are and not selling out. The actions you take line up with what you've told others about yourself.

Integrity is critical to a successful life. We all spend time building a reputation, an image of ourselves made up of what we like and what's important to us. When you act in a way that's consistent with that image, that's integrity.

In the movie *The Family Man*, there's a scene where a teenage girl buys a 99-cent soda and hands the store clerk a dollar. The clerk mistakes it for a ten-dollar bill – on purpose because he's testing her – and hands her back nine bucks. Of course, the right thing to do is to point out the mistake. She thinks about it for a second, and then takes the money and rushes out of the store.

She sold her integrity for nine dollars. How much is your integrity worth? How much would it take for you to compromise what you know to be right?

Live a life with integrity, and the possibilities are endless. People will trust you, and you can live with confidence, knowing that you are the person that you say you are. No ship may ever be unsinkable, but a life lived with integrity is pretty close!

TIP: Stick to what you believe, and don't sell out.

Success Building Tip 6

INTEGRITY, PART 2: THERE ARE NO SECRETS

Wouldn't it be fun to be invisible? You wouldn't have to change out of your PJs in the morning, you could do the Funky Chicken in public anytime you want, and no more embarrassing Facebook photos! But you could also sneak into places you don't belong and break all kinds of laws. The only thing stopping you would be your integrity.

The toughest tests of your integrity are the moments when you think no one will discover what you did. Like when you could leave a mean anonymous comment online. Or when you could take that pack of gum while the clerk is busy in the back.

Your values are the core of who you are, and every time you betray them, you're waging a war on yourself. You're attacking your own integrity. As it goes on, your conscience bears the burden of your actions. All of that inner turmoil will eventually show on the outside.

In the movie *A Knight's Tale*, our hero William

Thatcher would assess the damage to his armor after a long day of jousting. It would be riddled with pot holes and dings from all of the impact he endured. We may not show that type of outward damage, but it's instead a look of guilt, a distant distraction, shame, and a fear of disappointing the people around you.

But sometimes, the damage shows right away. If you're like me, you've discovered that secrets might not be as secret as we think. Maybe you thought you had covered all your tracks, or you were absolutely, positively certain that no one was watching. All you have to do is search for 'dumb criminals' online to find countless people who could've sworn they were going to get away with it.

Remember that there is a consequence for every action. Act with integrity, no matter the situation, no matter who you think is watching and who is actually watching. If you do that, you can live with a conscience so clear, it's practically invisible.

TIP: True integrity is shown in how you act when no one is watching.

Success Building Tip 7

INTEGRITY, PART 3: YOU'RE NOT ALONE

Who Wants to Be a Millionaire? I know the answer to that question: everyone! Except billionaires, I guess. So, most everyone!

On the show, it's great that if you're stumped on a question, you can phone a friend to help you answer it. Two heads are better than one. Integrity's the same way. If you need help sticking to your values and making the right choices, you can turn to a friend. Here's a plan:

1. **Find a friend.** Before you find yourself in a sticky situation, choose a friend who will help you. Find one whose opinion you respect, someone who will honor your privacy, someone who has your best interests in mind. Ask if you can talk to them regularly about it.
2. **Talk to them regularly!** Meet or talk with this friend often, going over the difficult situations that you find yourself in and the choices that you're faced with.
3. **Sound the 'alone alarm'.** I you're alone in a moment of crisis, phone your friend.

Accept their advice and encouragement, and remember that you don't have to face a crisis alone.

Also, it sounds obvious, but **tell the truth!** It doesn't do any good to have a friend to tell about your struggles if you act like you don't have any! "Oh, everything is going fine...Actually, better than fine! I'm perfect!"

The next time you feel alone in sticking with your values, phone a friend for accountability. Maybe you won't win a million bucks, but you'll feel like it!

TIP: Your closest friends can help you live a life of integrity.

Success Building Tip 8

FAITH, PART 1: BELIEVE

"Faith is believing in something when common sense tells you not to." – Fred Gailey, *Miracle on 34th Street*

Common sense is a good thing. It tells you to look both ways before crossing the street. It tells you not to wear peanut butter deodorant when hiking through the woods. Common sense wants evidence before believing something, but we can't always have evidence. That's where faith comes in.

Faith is the strong, steady belief in something without proof that thing should be believed in. Faith comes in many forms, like having trust in a person. When you go to the doctor, you have faith that he/she will know the best way to get you better. Or you can have faith in yourself and your abilities, that you have it takes to achieve your goal. There's no proof that you'll reach your dream, but you believe it will happen.

When most people think of faith, they think of believing that God exists and that He blesses and cares for us. I've heard this said about faith: *It's the substance of things hoped for, and evidence of those things not seen.* Even without seeing what the future looks like, I believe that my hopes are possible, and I live my life as such. Without seeing God, I know He's there for me.

I think most people would agree that faith is foundational for any person who desires to build a successful life. You'll have to believe in something even if you don't have the hard evidence for it. It's a scary leap to take, but one you have to do to land on success!

TIP: Ask yourself, "What do I have faith in?"

FAITH, PART 2: THE REASON

Every October, I watch *It's the Great Pumpkin, Charlie Brown*. Linus has deep faith in the Great Pumpkin: he writes letters to it, he misses trick-or-treating to see it, and he even falls asleep outside waiting for it. Linus just wanted to see the Great Pumpkin, but he was actually teaching us a good lesson about faith!

It's important to have faith, but it's just as important to know why you place your faith in what you believe in. Linus believed in the Great Pumpkin. Why? Did he know the Great Pumpkin? Did he hear stories about how great the Great Pumpkin was?

Too often, people just believe in something without knowing why they believe in it. That's called "blind faith." Maybe they do because it's the popular thing – what all their friends believe in. Or maybe someone they admire, like a celebrity, believes it.

Having blind faith makes it difficult to live a successful life. For example, would it be a good idea to have blind faith when going skydiving? No! You'd you want to know all about the skydiving company first, like if they're experienced, if they take the necessary safety precautions, and if they know how to pack parachutes so that they open when you need them to. You'd want to know why you believe in the skydiving company before jumping out of that airplane.

I have faith in God, and I know why I do. It's because of what I've read in the Bible, what I've learned about Him from other people, and what I've seen Him do in my life and the lives of others. Because I know why I believe in God, I don't constantly question my faith, and it's become a solid foundation for my life.

Don't just depend on blind faith. Whether you believe in pumpkins or parachutes – or anything else – get yourself to see why you believe it!

TIP: *Know what you believe in and why.*

Success Building Tip 10

FAITH, PART 3: TRIALS

"Consider it pure joy, my brothers, whenever you face trials of many kinds, because you know that the testing of your faith develops perseverance."
– James, The Bible

If I were to meet James today, I'd say,"AGHHH!" because he died about 2000 years ago, and I'd think he was a zombie. After I was sure he wasn't a zombie, I'd respectfully ask him, "Say what, James? Facing trials of many kinds doesn't sound like my idea of a joyful time." But as I think about it now, I understand what he meant.

When we start believing in something, that faith is weak. If you gave me a chair and said, "Stand on this chair," I wouldn't do it because I'd have a weak faith in it. I'd be afraid that it would collapse as soon as I put weight on it. But if I owned the chair for a month, and sat in it everyday, that's putting my faith to the test. I'm testing to see if I really trust the chair to hold my weight. And then one day, I might put one foot on it to test my faith a little more. Eventually, I'd give my faith in the chair a final exam and carefully stand on it with two feet. By testing my faith in the chair and sticking with it, I've grown my weak faith into a strong one.

When difficult times come in life and you hold to your faith, that's when it grows into a strong faith. Good times won't grow your faith because believing is easy when everything is going right. Keeping your faith in the face of a challenge is where the strengthening occurs.

Look at Bethany Hamilton, a professional surfer from Hawaii. When she was only 13, she was attacked by a shark and had her left arm torn off. That tragedy could have broken her faith – the faith she had in herself as a surfer and the faith she had in God to take care of her – and she could have quit surfing forever. But instead, she let her faith be strengthened by this trial, and she returned to surfing less than a month after the attack! Just a couple of years later, she won a national surfing competition!

When difficult trials pop up, don't let them break your faith. It's not easy, but take joy in the fact that your faith is growing stronger as you persevere through them. A strong faith can handle any challenge, even zombies!

TIP: Trials and tests make your faith stronger.

Success Building Tip *11*

HOPE: I'VE GOT A FEELING

Hope is sweet-minded and sweet-eyed. It draws pictures; it weaves fancies; it fills the future with delight. – Henry Ward Beecher

If you talk to anyone who's just bought a puppy, I doubt many people would say, "Oh boy...I get to have my furniture chewed on, my legs scratched, my hands bitten, and my carpets ruined." No – they would feel happy about their cute purchase! That's because they have hope.

Hope is the feeling of expecting something good to happen, an optimistic feeling. When people buy a puppy, or most baby pets, they expect that the animal will grow to become a loyal and loving part of the family. They have hope that owning that pet will make their lives happier, not worse. Otherwise, why buy something that just makes life harder?

To live a successful life, you need to live with hope, with the expectation that life will get even better. Even if you feel like you're at the bottom of the barrel and everything that could possibly go wrong has, you can focus on rising up. I like how Oscar Wilde said, "We are all in the gutter, but some of us are looking at the stars." Actually, at the bottom, they only place you *can* go is up!

When you have hope, here are some thoughts that you live by:

- I will do what I love to do.
- My dreams can come true.
- Even when I fail, I will learn from it.
- My friends and family will increase.
- I will grow in maturity and wisdom.
- Human culture will advance to make a better world.
- I will make a difference in the lives of others.

Those are definitely worth getting out of bed in the morning. Wherever you are in life, live with hope!

TIP: Everyday, remember that life will get even better. Enjoy the ride!

Success Building Tip 12

BOLDNESS: GOING FOR IT

Basketball legend Michael Jordan, American leader Dwight D. Eisenhower, and renowned actor Patrick Stewart (Charles Xavier, Captain Jean-Luc Picard) make good examples of successful lives. Even though their accomplishments are so different, they have at least one thing in common – something that shines forth among the crowd: baldness. Oops! I mean boldness.

Boldness is the willingness to do things that involve risk. It involves confidence and being able to pursue your goal in the face of fear.

Building a successful life can be scary sometimes, like when you have to take a risk or there's a ton of pressure to perform. Fear is natural, so you don't have to feel ashamed of feeling afraid in those situations. The key is what you do in the face of that fear.

You could stay in your comfort zone and avoid the moment. You *could* keep doing that time after time, and just live a plain life with no dreams, not following what you feel like you were made to do. That's life – just not a successful one.

Or you could have boldness! Face your fear, acknowledge the risk of losing, failing, or embarrassment, and go for it anyway.

Michael Jordan took the last shot with the game on the line, time and time again. Patrick Stewart performed "A Christmas Carol" on Broadway – all by himself! And before he was president, Eisenhower led the D-Day invasion of World War II.

In the face of adversity, remember our bold (and bald) heroes!

TIP: Face your fears and boldly go forward!

Success Building Tip 13

SELF-ESTEEM: YOU. ARE. AMAZING.

You are as amazing as you let yourself be. –
Elizabeth Alraune

What if you found out that I had a bicycle that
could fly, like in E.T.? And then what if I told you
that I've never flown with it, not even once?
You'd think that was crazy! What a waste to not
use my flying bike to, well, fly! That's what life is
like when you have low self-esteem.

Self-esteem is the level of confidence you have
in your own abilities and potential. When you
have a healthy self-esteem, you know that you
have what it takes to achieve your goals, even
if you have a long road to get there. You are
happy with the person you are, and you feel
good about sharing who you are with others.

Having a low self-esteem is a common problem
for people of all ages. When you have it, you
have a poor opinion of yourself. You think that
you're not good enough to reach your dreams,
and that you're not very significant in the world.
Just so I'm clear: THAT'S A LIE! But when you

have low self-esteem, you don't recognize the lie.

A low self-esteem would tell me that drawing with chalk on a black bedsheet is a strange career, and that it's something I shouldn't be proud of. It would tell me that I am a weird person. A healthy self-esteem tells me that I'm using the gifts that God gave me to entertain and encourage people around the world. It tells me that I should be happy about who I am. It tells me that though I may not be a lot of things in this world, I am a unique person (who's weird) and that there's no one else like me.

Your self-esteem is the starting point for many of your decisions, so make sure yours is healthy. Embrace the fact that you are truly unique and that there are no others like you and you have great things to offer. That's when things (maybe even bikes) can really take off!

TIP: Stop worrying about what everyone else has. Have confidence in yourself and your abilities.

Success Building Tip 14

HUMILITY: OTHERS FIRST

Humility is not thinking less of yourself; it's thinking of yourself less. - Rick Warren

There are three people that I can't stop thinking about – how they're feeling, what they're doing, what other people think of them. Wouldn't it be nice if I were talking about my family? However, I'm talking about me, myself, and I.

We think about ourselves a little too much. Throughout the day, we dwell on the things we want to buy, the people we want to meet, or the places we want to go. True success requires that you occasionally take the focus off of yourself and place it on others. That's humility.

Humility is the thinking that other people are just as important as you are. It's the opposite of being arrogant or prideful. The humble person will hold a door open so that someone else can go in first. The humble person doesn't take the biggest piece of pie, leaving it for another to enjoy. And the humble person doesn't exploit others for his own gain.

Just because you're humble doesn't mean that you won't stand out. I think it's the opposite. People are drawn to a humble person because that person makes them feel important. I like how Charles de Montesquieu put it: ""To become truly great, one has to stand with people, not above them."

The funny thing is that when I think of others first, I find that I am blessed by being a blessing to others. It's a win-win situation!

TIP: Think about the needs and comfort of others first.

Success Building Tip 15

BEING CONTENT: FOCUS ON YOUR OWN GRASS

I always thought it would be fun to grow up to be a fireman or an astronaut, or a Twinkie tester, but you know who I really wanted to be? Scrooge McDuck! I'd like a huge vault of gold coins to swim in, though I've always wondered what it would feel like to dive into that million-dollar pool. (Probably a lot like getting your nose smashed in.)

I'm all grown up now, and I never got to be Scrooge McDuck. But that's okay because I am content.

Being content is having satisfaction and happiness in the circumstances of your life. You feel pleased with the school or job you're in, the house where you live, or the things that you own.

Being content doesn't mean that you can't strive for better circumstances. By all means, work toward higher grades or try to get that promotion. Save money for that large LEGO kit.

But while your eyes are on the prize, make sure you appreciate what you have, and enjoy the moment.

If you think, "The grass is always greener on the other side," it's usually a sign of *not* being content. You're focusing on what your neighbors have, thinking that they always have it better. But the funny thing is that most times, the neighbors are thinking the same thing about you! The grass isn't *always* greener on the other side (unless you have a dirt backyard, which would make an awesome mud pit to play in, by the way).

Take time to remember the good things you have. Living a content life is so much better than worrying about what you don't have. If Scrooge McDuck's own relatives can be happy swimming and eating bread at the park, then I can be happy with my life!

TIP: Life is good; appreciate it!

Success Building Tip 16

DEPENDABILITY: DELIVERING RESULTS

Let's say that I needed to know how to take care of a monkey, and I needed to know NOW. Well, thanks to Google, I can just type in "how to take care of a monkey" and get all the info I need. Google works the same way every time, and I know that when I type in 'google.com', that it's going to come up waiting for my next search. For me, Google is dependable.

When you're **dependable**, it means that people can trust you to do what you're supposed to do. You achieve dependability by consistently delivering results. There's no second-guessing whether you'll get the job done.

Dependability means that your friends, classmates, co-workers – the people who know you – are *able* to *depend* on you. So, your classmates can trust you to do your part of the project. And your boss can rely on you to do the job she's paying you to do. And your spouse doesn't have to worry that you're going to bring home a monkey you found hanging from a tree in the park.

We all know what it feels like when someone lets you down. There's disappointment, anxiety, and anger. Even the most dependable person you know will let you down once in a while. When that happens, the dependable person tries to right the wrong, whether it's with an apology or trying again, and they work to recapture that quality of being dependable.

It would be nice if finding a dependable person were as easy as searching on Google, but the truth is finding someone who is dependable these days can be a rare find. Fortunately, you can choose to have dependability for everyone else around you!

TIP: Being dependable is a big part of being successful.

Success Building Tip 17

KINDNESS: IT'S GOLDEN

DO NOT ENTER. LEFT TURN ONLY. NO CELL PHONE USE.

There are lots of rules in this world. Some are painted on big metal signs, like STOP. Others are unwritten, like "Do not tap dance on your teacher's desk during class." But there's one rule so valuable that it's called the Golden Rule: **Do unto others as you would have them do unto you.** In other words, treat everyone the way you want them to treat you. That's the foundation of kindness.

Kindness is the quality of being warm, polite, and compassionate toward others. Kindness takes so many forms that I could devote a whole book to it and just scratch the surface. Kindness is mowing your neighbor's lawn when he's sick, congratulating your friend on getting the part in the play, and taking your mom to dinner.

Zig Ziglar, one of the country's most renowned motivational leaders says, "If you go looking for a friend, you're going to find they're very scarce.

If you go out to be a friend, you'll find them everywhere."

Have you ever wondered why it's called the Golden Rule and not the Silver Rule or Bronze Rule? It's because gold is most valuable, and when you extend kindness to others – when you set aside selfishness, and replace it with selflessness – the return on your investment is solid gold.

All of us want to be treated with kindness. When you eat at a restaurant, you want the server to smile at you instead of scowl. When you make a mistake at work, would you rather have the boss yell at you or encourage you to do better?

The Golden Rule works because most everyone wants the same things in a relationship: respect, attention, and kindness. When you treat someone a certain way, they'll remember to treat you the same, and vice versa. Simply put, kindness inspires more kindness, and the world could always use more of that!

TIP: Being kind to others is always a good investment.

Success Building Tip 18

SINCERITY: I REALLY MEAN IT

"Thanks a lot."

When I read that, it sounds one of two ways in my head:

1. I'd like to thank you a great deal. I appreciate it!
2. I'm being sarcastic. I don't appreciate it at all!

I think we've all heard someone say, "Thanks a lot," in a sarcastic way. Isn't it weird how one phrase can mean two completely opposite things? That's the difference between sincerity and sarcasm. Building a successful life brick-by-brick means sometimes you'll need to set aside the sarcasm to be sincere.

When you speak with **sincerity**, you honestly mean what you say; you're genuine. You say "thank you" because you actually appreciate something. "I'm so excited" means that you are really anticipating what's about to happen.

Sarcasm is when you say something, but you

mean the opposite. It's often a harsh, ironic comment. When someone says "I'm so excited" with sarcasm, they really mean that they don't care about what's going to happen; they may even be dreading it.

If you want a successful life, you don't want people second-guessing everything you say. They shouldn't have to wonder whether you meant what you said, or whether you meant the opposite. Sarcasm might get a quick laugh sometimes, but it's much more likely to hurt someone's feelings, damage your reputation, and be taken the wrong way. And it's confusing in the moments you're trying to be sincere if everyone is used to you being sarcastic.

It took me a long time to understand that there is a time and place for sarcasm, especially if you have a comedic mind like myself. However, sincerity is the key to helping people experience the real you.

Speak with sincerity, and people will learn more about you, understand you, and thank you – and they'll really mean it!

TIP: Avoid sarcasm when it's time to be sincere.

Success Building Tip 19

GENEROSITY: LIVE WITH AN OPEN HAND

"We make a living by what we get, but we make a life by what we give." - Winston Churchill

I confess that I've dreamed of winning the lottery. What would it be like to win, say, $11 million? There's a lot I would do that money – like buy 78,000 LEGO Millennium Falcon sets.

Allen and Violet Large won $11 million, and they had a different idea: Give it all away! Their generosity helped hospitals, churches, and charities in their corner of Canada. (Unfortunately, they forgot to send me a couple of Millennium Falcons.)

Generosity is the willingness to give away what you own to help others. We usually think of generosity in terms of money, but it goes beyond that. You can be generous with other things, like:

- **Your time**, by patiently listening to a friend share his/her thoughts.

- **Your talents**, by fixing a neighbor's computer if they're allergic to technology.
- **Your treasure**, by letting someone in need borrow your car.

I'm living proof of the good that generosity can do. Friends and mentors have selflessly given their time, talent, and treasure to help me achieve my dreams. And I know they were happy to do it. I know I feel that way when I'm able to give to someone else.

So, forget the lottery, and go for generosity instead. The more you give away, the richer you feel!

TIP: Be generous with what you have.

Success Building Tip 20

PUNCTUALITY: SET YOUR WATCH

One of my favorite movies scenes of all time is when Doc Brown tries to get Marty McFly back to the future in *Back to the Future*. If you've never seen the movie, stop reading this book, rent/borrow/buy the movie, watch it, and then come back here. I'll wait...

OK – Wasn't it a thrill ride when the lightning was about to strike the clock tower, and Doc was scrambling to get the cables connected? It looked like he wasn't going to make it, but he miraculously plugged it all in just as the lightning struck.

Doing things at the last nanosecond makes for great movie scenes, but that's not the kind of thrill ride you want when building a successful life. You need punctuality.

Punctuality is the ability to be somewhere or complete tasks by the appointed time. In other words: Don't be late! If you've agreed to meet someone at a certain time, being late shows disrespect to that person in at least two ways:

1. You're failing to do what you said you would do.
2. You're wasting the other person's time.

There's a saying that goes If *you're early, then you're on time*. If you're on time, then you're late. So, if you slide into the room at 3:59 and 59 seconds for your 4:00 meeting, you're technically on time. But I wouldn't recommend it.

Give yourself plenty of time to work with. If you find that you're regularly late, leave 15 minutes earlier than you think you need to leave. You never know when you might be delayed by traffic or your shoe falling off or a freak snowstorm in July.

Back to the Future would've been less thrilling if lightning was going to strike the clock tower again five minutes later. In the same way (sort of), you don't get a second chance to be on time, so get it right the first time!

TIP: Be early. Be early. Be early!

Success Building Tip 21

HUMOR: WHAT'S SO FUNNY?

Why did the chicken cross the road? To get to her car after a long day at the office!

Not very funny, huh? That's okay; I'm still confident in my sense of humor, and I want you to feel the same way about yours.

Humor is the quality of being amusing or comical. It's also the ability to understand when others are being humorous. Having a sense of humor isn't necessarily essential to a successful life, but it sure does help! Humor can make communication more fun. The best thing about having a sense of humor is that it's not hard work; just be yourself. Don't force yourself to tell jokes, and don't feel bad if you don't get someone else's jokes (especially brilliant ones about poultry commuting home after work).

The one bit of work when it comes to humor is this: Use common sense. Humor is a wonderful thing, but when used in the wrong way or at the wrong time, it can be hurtful. So, before you tell a joke, simply run through this 35-point checklist to make sure it's appropriate:

Just kidding! Here are two things to remember, though: Humility and Kindness (as mentioned earlier in the book). Humility reminds us that everyone is equally important and worthy of respect. Kindness teaches us that we should treat each other the way that we want to be treated. And throw Good Timing in there, too. If your teacher is upset at you over something, you probably shouldn't put on a rubber clown nose to try to make him laugh.

I hope your sense of humor can drive you to success! (Speaking of driving, what if I told you the hen drives a Mini COOPer? You know, like a chicken coop? HENda Accord?)

TIP: Feel free to use your sense of humor, with lots of common sense.

Success Building Tip 22

VISION, PART 1: THE IMAGE

I'm standing on stage in front of a symphony orchestra with a huge blank canvas. The crowd is ready to see one of the most inspiring visual presentations ever. As a powerful movie score fills the room, I begin to Speedscape – a.k.a. drawing as fast as I can, praying to God it looks like something. Each stroke on the canvas is perfectly choreographed to every note played.

That amazing scene hasn't happened in my life, but I'm sure it will someday. It's my vision.

I define **vision** as a vivid mental image of what's possible. It's not a dream; it's a reality that has yet to come into existence.

We all need a mental image of what's possible in our lives. Without one, it might feel like you're wandering through life with no goal or direction. The good news is that it's not hard to create your vision.

To do that, just think about all the possibilities and potential in your life. What do you see yourself working towards? Maybe it's walking across the stage at graduation, or it's getting hired for the perfect job. Maybe it's the cover of your first book or hearing your song on the radio.

Everyone is capable of creating a vision of their future. Just picture it in your mind to see where you're headed!

TIP: Envision your goals, and go after them!

Success Building Tip 23

VISION, PART 2: THE QUEST

I had just finished speaking about ADHD and other learning challenges at a school when a student came up to me and blurted out, "I can't read." I told her how sorry I was to hear this because books are full of great knowledge and new ideas.

"Have you ever tried reading?" I asked. And she said no!

To have a successful life, it's key to have a vision, but you don't stop there. A vision inspires and motivates you to go on a quest to pursue it. In other words, **you have to try**. That's the only way your vision will become a reality.

When I said "quest," you might have pictured yourself dressing up in camping gear, flying to South America, and hacking your way through the jungle to pursue your vision. But you don't have to do that at all – unless you envision discovering lost Mayan treasures. A **quest** is a dedicated and relentless pursuit to make your vision a reality.

Anyone can go on a quest, and it can happen anywhere, regardless of your skills with a machete. A quest is the single mom who goes to night school to get an education because she sees herself with a better life. A quest is the businessman risking everything because he already sees his business taking off. As you'd imagine, a quest isn't a quick and easy trip, but your vision will inspire you along the way.

If you see your vision, just don't enjoy the view. Start pursuing it!

TIP: Go on a quest to achieve your vision.

Success Building Tip 24

INSPIRATION: WHERE IDEAS COME FROM

Have you ever sat down to start writing a report, blog post, or even an email, and found that the words aren't flowing? That's called writer's block. But writers aren't the only unlucky ones. All kinds of people, like musicians, chefs, and athletes, can feel like they don't have the mental energy to get going. I can stare at a blank canvas for hours before getting the foggiest notion of what I want to create. What we all need is inspiration.

Inspiration is the process of acquiring the creative ideas that make up your vision. Let's say you have a vision of publishing a book. Your quest will begin with the writing, but what will you write about? Inspiration helps you come up with those ideas.

Sometimes you have to seek out inspiration. Here are some tips on where to find it:

1. **Dive in.** There's a saying that "you are what you eat." I believe you are also what you read, listen to, etc., so if you're writing

a book, then read good books. If you're composing songs, listen to good music. From that healthy diet, good ideas will flow.

2. **Talk to inspiring people.** We're affected by the people around us whether or not we realize it. You might as well surround yourself with people who will lift you up and get the best out of you.

3. **Don't listen to the naysayers.** And just like #2, watch out the people who can rob you of joy, freedom, and creativity. Often your worst critic is you, so don't listen to self-created negativity and sarcasm.

Whether you have to get around, go over, or plow through, don't let a block stop you!

TIP: Seek out inspiration to let the ideas flow.

Success Building Tip 25

INITIATIVE: BE A SELF-STARTER

Several years ago, my speaking schedule started filling up, so I decided to bring on a summer intern. I've always felt that giving students an experience outside of their normal routine helps them think about the future in new ways. An internship with me for a summer would do just that, because there was no normal routine. One week we might be flying out to Colorado and the next week driving to Wisconsin. My intern would learn new skills, meet new people, and travel to new places. However, for my intern to maximize the fullness of this experience, he would need one thing: initiative.

Initiative is the ability to assess and start tasks independently. Since my summer schedule was so busy and it was just the two of us, I needed my intern to assess a situation, think of a solution, and act on it, all on his own. If I had to constantly tell him what to do, it would be more work than it was worth. And that's what happened the first month.

My intern didn't show a single ounce of

initiative, and I quickly began to regret ever coming up with the idea. But then I learned that all of the jobs he'd had in the past were directed by others. This was the first time he was challenged to think for himself and do as he thought best. In the end, all he needed was a green light to take initiative, and the rest of that summer was a joy.

Growing up, we're told what, when, and how to do everything. This is fine as you learn and develop new skills, but at some point, you need to use your knowledge and experience to take initiative.

Taking initiative is key to building success. It tells the world that you are confident, determined, and willing to work!

TIP: When it comes to taking initiative... there's always a green light.

Success Building Tip 26

PREPAREDNESS: READY FOR WHAT'S NEXT

Batman chases the villain down a dark alleyway. The bad guy shoots, but Batman is safe under his Bat-Armor. They enter a pitch black warehouse, but Batman has his Bat-Flashlight. Then the bad guy slips out and hops in a getaway car! No problem; Batman reaches for his Bat-Throwing Stars to pop the tires and... they're not here? What?! He tries another spot on his utility belt. Nope. While Batman searches, the bad guy speeds away.

I guarantee that's something you'll NEVER see in a Batman movie because:

1. that would just be a lame action sequence and
2. Batman has preparedness.

Preparedness is defined as the state of being ready. Preparedness helps you pursue your vision because it enables you to effectively handle the tasks, challenges, and opportunities in life. There are two kinds of preparedness that I think are key: being ready for the expected and being ready for the unexpected.

Being ready for the expected means that you have a commitment, and you do the necessary work ahead of time to make it succeed. It's putting in the hours to study for a big test. Or it's researching the company before you go in for the job interview.

Being ready for the unexpected means that you address the challenges that could pop up, but probably won't. It's keeping an umbrella in your backpack so you don't get caught in the rain. And it's having jumper cables in the trunk in case your car battery dies. It's also being ready for an opportunity, like keeping your business cards in your wallet.

To be prepared, you don't NEED a utility belt with an umbrella, jumper cables, and a stack of business cards. (But if you make one, please send me a photo!) Just think ahead, and prepare yourself!

TIP: Prepare for the expected and the unexpected.

Success Building Tip 27

ORGANIZATION: EVERYTHING HAS A HOME

I love a good scavenger hunt. It's fun to pick up on clues and stretch your mind to figure out where the prizes are hidden. It's the thrill of the search! Except when you're in a hurry and you can't find your keys and wallet. That's when organization can save the day.

Organization is the state of arranging items in a consistent and orderly manner. When you're organized, the things you need are where they're supposed to be when you need them.

Organization affects you all day, every day. In the morning, you start in the bathroom and use all kinds of brushes, gels, and goops to get ready. And then on to the kitchen full of boxes, cans, bottles, plates, bowls, and silverware. Then you collect your keys, glasses, wallet, phone, and bags to go out. How frustrating would it be if you had to search for what you needed at every point of that process? (I've been there, done that, and it stinks!)

Think of it this way: Everything should have a

home. You may need to buy shelves and boxes and trays, but it's money well spent. So, every time you need your keys, you'll just go to their home to find them. And you'll be less likely to lose things, so you won't need to buy two or more of something you already have.

The time and money you save from organizing can go directly toward pursuing your vision. And by preventing frustration, you'll have a lot more mental energy to devote, too.

Save the scavenger hunt for the next birthday party. Being organized is like finding hidden treasure everyday...without having to find anything hidden, because all your stuff is at home. So, I guess being organized is more like having treasures right out in the open, no hunting, no finding. You just grab it and go!

TIP: Give everything a home and keep it there.

Success Building Tip 28

FLEXIBILITY: PLANS CHANGE

I was getting ready to present at a festival when they asked me to cut my speaking time down from 45 minutes. I figured I could trim a few things if it would help everyone out. But they wanted more and more, and before I knew it, I only had 15 minutes to work with! Instead of fighting it, I chose to be flexible.

Flexibility is the ability to manage unexpected circumstances and willingly change your plans. At the festival, I could have gotten upset at having my time slashed, but instead I decided to give 'em the best 15 minutes I had!

Pursuing your vision is like driving a car: a setback could be right around the corner. Flexibility allows you to find a detour around these setbacks instead of just grinding to a halt. It just takes patience and a willingness to change your plans.

If you want a website but can't pay a designer, try to work out a trade. If you're making brownies but don't have any oil, use applesauce.

If your camera batteries die while you're out, take pictures with your phone.

When George Lucas was looking for an actor to play Han Solo in *Star Wars*, he hired Harrison Ford to help with the auditions. After months of auditions, he couldn't find the right actor, so he let Ford try out for it. Of course, Harrison won the part and the rest is history.

There is usually a way to turn a negative circumstance into a positive one. You just have to be flexible to find it!

TIP: Be willing to change your plans.

Success Building Tip 29

ENDURANCE: PUSH THROUGH THE TOUGH TIMES

Life can be tough, especially when you're pursuing your vision. One author faced one adversity after another while writing her first book. Her mother died. She got married and had a baby, and then got divorced. And she lost her job. She submitted the book to 12 different publishers, and they all rejected it.

A small publisher finally took a chance on her, and that's how Harry Potter was introduced to the world. Most people would have stopped writing during those tough times, but J.K. Rowling endured.

Endurance is the ability to work through a time of difficult situations. Last time we talked about having flexibility and finding detours when setbacks occur. But sometimes there aren't any detours; you just have to go through it.

There might be a heavy load, like the work just piles up. Or the going may be slow and things aren't moving as quickly as you'd like. Or the road may be rocky as personal situations get in the way.

To get through these tough times, you'll have to rely on your values. Depending on the situation, you might need to dig deep and call upon your Faith, work to find Hope, be Bold in the face of adversity, or rely on your positive Self-esteem to keep moving forward. You'll need to look upon your vision to remind you of where you're headed. And you may seek more Inspiration for new ideas.

J.K. Rowling is living a modern rags-to-riches story. When we endure, there's no telling what kind of magic is possible!

TIP: When you can't get around setbacks, push through and endure.

Success Building Tip 30

SUCCESS: AFTER YOU CROSS THE FINISH LINE

I was watching the 100 meter dash, and I saw something amazing – other than the sight of these guys running the length of a football field in 10 seconds. The winner went around and hugged the other runners, even his rival. He could have strutted around the track like a peacock and then run out for tacos, but he seemed to handle success well.

I thought about what it took for the sprinters to make it to the big race. The vision, the preparation, the training, the setbacks, the endurance. It sounds a lot like you pursuing your vision, doesn't it?

In your pursuit, **success** is achieving your vision so that it becomes a reality. When your goal is reached, and what a sweet moment that will be, the next thing that might pop in your head is, "What's next?"

Well, here's a few ideas on how to handle your success:

1. Celebrate with others. Victory is great, but it's even better when you share it. You had

people support you along the way; party with them. And don't forget about Humility!

2. Reward yourself. There's nothing wrong with treating yourself a little, too! Reward yourself on all of your hard work and endurance. Maybe an ice cream sundae, or three.

3. Debrief. Think about the steps you took to achieve success. Jot down anything insightful about the journey before you forget. It'll probably come in handy.

4. Rest. Take a break and get renewed and refreshed.

5. Start envisioning again. I hope you didn't think you were finished! As long as you're alive, you should always be pursuing a vision. It may be short-term, like writing a song, or it can be a journey, like moving to another country. A vision inspires hope, and hope inspires life.

Whether it's running on a track or running for office, I hope you succeed in making your vision a reality. And then the next one, too! And the one after that...

TIP: Celebrate your success with humility and start working toward the next one.

NOTES

NOTES